50 Interview Questions with Answers for AI ML Engineer Position

Welcome to "Mastering the Interview: 50 Essential Questions for AI/ML Engineers." In today's rapidly evolving technological landscape, the demand for skilled AI and ML professionals is soaring. As organizations increasingly rely on data-driven insights and intelligent systems, the role of AI/ML engineers has become pivotal in driving innovation and shaping the future.

This book aims to equip aspiring AI/ML engineers with the knowledge and confidence they need to excel in interviews. Whether you are a fresh graduate embarking on your career journey or an experienced professional seeking new opportunities, this comprehensive collection of interview questions will help you sharpen your technical acumen, reinforce your understanding of key concepts, and showcase your expertise in the field of artificial intelligence and machine learning.

Interviews can be daunting, especially when the stakes are high and competition is fierce. Understanding the specific areas of focus and the types of questions typically asked can give you a distinct advantage. Our carefully curated list of 50 interview questions covers a wide range of topics and techniques relevant to AI and ML, ensuring that you are well-prepared to tackle any interview scenario.

Each question in this book is designed to delve deep into the fundamentals of AI and ML, providing you with an opportunity to showcase your problem-solving skills, analytical thinking, and domain knowledge. We go beyond the basic theoretical concepts and delve into real-world scenarios, ensuring that you are not only well-versed in theory but also capable of applying your knowledge to practical challenges.

While the questions in this book provide a solid foundation for interview preparation, it is important to note that the goal is not simply to memorize answers. Instead, we encourage you to grasp the underlying principles and develop a comprehensive understanding of the subject matter. This will enable you to approach interview questions with confidence and demonstrate your ability to think critically, adapt to new challenges, and communicate effectively.

To further enhance your learning experience, each question is accompanied by a detailed answer that explains the concepts, methodologies, and best practices involved. This will help you deepen your understanding and gain valuable insights that can be applied to both interview scenarios and real-world AI/ML projects.

In addition to technical knowledge, we also emphasize the importance of soft skills. Throughout the book, we provide guidance on effective communication, teamwork, and problem-solving strategies. These skills are crucial for AI/ML engineers, as they often work collaboratively with cross-functional teams and need to effectively articulate their ideas and findings.

"Mastering the Interview: 50 Essential Questions for AI/ML Engineers" is your comprehensive guide to preparing for AI/ML interviews. By diligently studying and practicing the questions in this book, you will gain the confidence and expertise needed to succeed in the highly competitive world of AI and ML.

Remember, preparation is the key to success. So, dive in, explore the questions, and embark on your journey to becoming a sought-after AI/ML engineer. Good luck!

Let the interviewing begin.

Best regards,

Explain the concept of supervised learning.

Supervised learning is a type of machine learning algorithm that is used to learn from labeled training data. The goal of supervised learning is to build a model that can make predictions about new data, based on the patterns it has learned from the training data.

Artificial intelligence (AI) is a branch of computer science that deals with the creation of intelligent agents, which are systems that can reason, learn, and act autonomously. AI research deals with the question of how to create computers that are capable of intelligent behaviour.

Machine learning is a subfield of AI that deals with the question of how to create computer systems that can learn from data, and improve their performance at tasks over time. Machine learning algorithms are used to build models that can automatically learn and improve from experience.

What is unsupervised learning, and when is it used?

Unsupervised learning is a type of machine learning algorithm that is used to find patterns in data. It is used when the data is not labeled and there is no ground truth to be learned. The goal of unsupervised learning is to find hidden structure in the data. Artificial intelligence is a field of computer science that deals with the creation of intelligent agents, which are systems that can reason, learn, and act autonomously. Machine learning is a subset of artificial intelligence that deals with the creation of algorithms that can learn from data.

Describe the process of feature selection and its importance in machine learning.

The process of feature selection is a crucial part of machine learning. It is the process of choosing the most relevant features from a dataset to train a model. This is important because it can help to improve the accuracy of the model and reduce the training time.

There are a number of different methods that can be used for feature selection. One popular method is called recursive feature elimination. This method starts with all of the features in the dataset and then removes the least important features one by one. This process is repeated until only the most important features are left.

Another popular method is called random forest. This method creates a number of different decision trees. Each tree is trained on a different subset of the data. The features that are most important for the trees are the ones that are most important for the overall model.

Feature selection is an important part of machine learning because it can help to improve the accuracy of the model. It is also important because it can reduce the training time.

What are the key steps involved in a machine learning project?

There are key steps involved in any machine learning project, no matter what the specific application may be. The first step is to gather data. This data can come from a variety of sources, but it must be clean and organized in a way that the machine can understand. Once the data is gathered, it must be processed and analyzed to look for patterns. The machine learning algorithm is then applied to the data in order to learn from it. Finally, the results of the machine learning project are evaluated and monitored to ensure that the desired results are being achieved.

The difference between artificial intelligence and machine learning is that artificial intelligence is a field of study that deals with the creation of intelligent agents, which are systems that can reason and make decisions on their own. Machine learning, on the other hand, is a subset of artificial intelligence that deals specifically with the ability of machines to learn from data.

How do you handle missing data in a dataset?

There are a few ways to handle missing data in a dataset. One way is to simply delete the rows or columns that contain missing data. This is not always the best option, as it can lead to a loss of information. Another way to handle missing data is to impute the missing values. This can be done by using a mean or median value for numerical data, or by using the most common value for categorical data. Another option is to use a predictive model to estimate the missing values. This is usually done with machine learning algorithms.

What is the purpose of regularization in machine learning algorithms?

The purpose of regularization in machine learning algorithms is to prevent overfitting. Overfitting occurs when a model is too complex and captures too much detail, resulting in poor generalization and poor performance on new data. Regularization helps to simplify the model and improve generalization.

Artificial intelligence is a field of computer science and engineering focused on the creation of intelligent agents, which are systems that can reason, learn, and act autonomously. Machine learning is a subfield of AI that deals with the design and development of algorithms that can learn from data.

Explain the bias-variance tradeoff in machine learning.

Artificial intelligence (AI) is a field of computer science that aims to create intelligent agents, which are systems that can reason, learn, and act autonomously. Machine learning (ML) is a subfield of AI that deals with the construction of algorithms that can learn from data.

The bias-variance tradeoff is a fundamental problem in machine learning. The tradeoff is between two types of error that can occur when a model is trained on data: bias and variance. Bias is the error that is introduced by making assumptions about the data that are not true. Variance is the error that is introduced by the variability of the data.

The goal of any machine learning algorithm is to minimize both bias and variance. However, it is usually not possible to completely eliminate both types of error. This tradeoff is known as the bias-variance tradeoff.

There are two main ways to reduce bias:

1. Use a more flexible model. This will allow the model to fit the data better, but it may also increase the variance.

2. Use more data. This will allow the model to better learn the underlying patterns in the data, and it will also reduce the variance.

There are two main ways to reduce variance:

1. Use a less flexible model. This will make the model less sensitive to the variability in the data, but it may also increase the bias.

2. Use regularization. This is a technique that penalizes the model for having large weights. This will make the model less sensitive to the variability in the data, and it will also reduce the variance.

What is overfitting, and how can it be prevented?

Overfitting is when a model is too specific to the training data, and does not generalize well to new data. This can be prevented by using cross-validation, which is a technique for assessing how the results of a statistical model will generalize to an independent data set.

Artificial intelligence is a branch of computer science that deals with creating intelligent agents, which are systems that can reason, learn, and act autonomously. Machine learning is a subset of artificial intelligence that deals with the creation of algorithms that can learn from and make predictions on data.

What evaluation metrics would you use to assess a classification model's performance?

There are many different evaluation metrics that can be used to assess a classification model's performance. Some common metrics include accuracy, precision, recall, and F1 score. It is important to choose the right metric for the task at hand, as different metrics can emphasize different aspects of the model's performance. For example, accuracy is a good metric to use if the goal is to have a model that makes as few mistakes as possible. However, if the goal is to have a model that can detect all instances of a certain class, then recall would be a better metric to use.

Artificial intelligence (AI) is a branch of computer science that deals with creating intelligent agents, which are systems that can reason, learn, and act autonomously. Machine learning (ML) is a subfield of AI that deals with the development of algorithms that allow machines to learn from data. ML algorithms are often used to create predictive models, which are used to make predictions about future events.

Describe the difference between bagging and boosting techniques in ensemble learning.

Bagging and boosting are two ensemble learning techniques that can be used to improve the performance of machine learning models. Both methods involve training multiple models and then combining the predictions of the individual models to make a final prediction.

Bagging is a technique that trains each model in the ensemble independently and then combines the predictions by taking the average. This can help to reduce the variance of the predictions and improve the overall accuracy of the ensemble.

Boosting is a technique that trains each model in the ensemble sequentially. The first model is trained on the entire dataset and then the second model is trained on the data that was misclassified by the first model. This process is repeated until all models are trained. The predictions of the individual models are then combined by taking the weighted average. This can help to reduce the bias of the predictions and improve the overall accuracy of the ensemble.

Explain the concept of gradient descent in optimization algorithms.

Gradient descent is an optimization algorithm used to find the local minimum of a function. It works by iteratively moving in the direction of the steepest descent until it reaches a point where the gradient is zero.

Artificial intelligence is a branch of computer science that deals with the creation of intelligent agents, which are systems that can reason, learn, and act autonomously. Machine learning is a subfield of artificial intelligence that deals with the development of algorithms that can learn from data and improve their performance over time.

How do you handle imbalanced datasets in machine learning?

When it comes to imbalanced datasets in machine learning, there are a few different ways to handle them. One way is to oversample the minority class or undersample the majority class. Another way is to use a technique called SMOTE (synthetic minority oversampling technique).

When it comes to the difference between artificial intelligence and machine learning, it is important to understand that artificial intelligence is a broader term that includes machine learning. Machine learning is a subset of artificial intelligence that deals with the ability of machines to learn from data.

What is the difference between precision and recall?

Precision and recall are two important measures of performance for machine learning models. Precision is a measure of how many of the items that the model predicts are actually correct. Recall is a measure of how many of the correct items the model predicts.

Artificial intelligence is a field of computer science that deals with creating intelligent agents, which are systems that can reason, learn, and act autonomously. Machine learning is a subfield of artificial intelligence that deals with the creation of algorithms that can learn from data.

Describe the purpose and functioning of a convolutional neural network (CNN).

A convolutional neural network (CNN) is a type of artificial intelligence that is used to process data with a grid-like structure, such as an image. CNNs are similar to traditional neural networks, but they are composed of a series of layers, each of which performs a convolution operation on the data. This allows CNNs to learn complex patterns in data and to make predictions about new data.

Machine learning is a type of artificial intelligence that is used to learn from data. Machine learning algorithms are able to automatically improve given more data. There are many different types of machine learning, including supervised learning, unsupervised learning, and reinforcement learning.

What is recurrent neural network (RNN) and where is it commonly used?

RNN is a type of artificial neural network where connections between nodes form a directed graph along a temporal sequence. This allows it to exhibit temporal dynamic behavior. Unlike traditional neural networks, which are limited to processing a fixed number of inputs, RNNs can process an arbitrary number of inputs, making them ideal for tasks that involve sequential data.

RNNs are commonly used in tasks such as language modeling and machine translation, where the order of the input data is important.

Explain the concept of transfer learning in deep learning.

Transfer learning is a deep learning technique that allows you to use knowledge from one task to improve performance on another task.

For example, you could use transfer learning to take a model trained on a dataset of images of cats and dogs and use it to create a new model that is better at classifying images of dogs.

The key difference between artificial intelligence and machine learning is that artificial intelligence is focused on creating intelligent machines that can perform tasks that are difficult or impossible for humans to do. Machine learning, on the other hand, is a subset of artificial intelligence that focuses on creating algorithms that can learn from data and improve their performance over time.

What is the difference between L1 and L2 regularization in neural networks?

L1 and L2 regularization are both methods used to prevent overfitting in neural networks. L1 regularization adds a penalty to the weights of the network based on the absolute value of the weights, while L2 regularization adds a penalty based on the square of the weights. Both methods help to prevent the network from overfitting to the training data, but L2 regularization is generally considered to be more effective.

Describe the concept of generative adversarial networks (GANs).

Generative adversarial networks (GANs) are a type of artificial intelligence (AI) that are used to generate new data from a given input. Machine learning is a subset of AI that deals with the ability of machines to learn from data and improve their performance over time. GANs are a type of machine learning that is used to generate new data from a given input.

How would you approach feature engineering for a given machine learning problem?

Artificial intelligence (AI) and machine learning (ML) are often used interchangeably, but there is a big difference between the two. AI is a process of programming a computer to make decisions for itself. This can be done through a number of methods, including rule-based systems, decision trees, and genetic algorithms. ML, on the other hand, is a process of teaching a computer to learn from data. This is usually done through a process of training a computer with a large dataset, and then testing it on a smaller dataset to see how accurately it can predict the correct output.

Explain the concept of dimensionality reduction. What techniques can be used for this purpose?

Dimensionality reduction is the process of reducing the number of variables in a data set. This can be done for a variety of reasons, including making the data more manageable, reducing noise, and improving the accuracy of machine learning models. There are a number of techniques that can be used for dimensionality reduction, including feature selection, feature extraction, and principal component analysis.

How does the backpropagation algorithm work in neural networks?

The backpropagation algorithm is a method used to train neural networks. It is a type of supervised learning, where the desired output is known in advance. The algorithm adjusts the weights of the connections between the neurons in the network so that the output of the network is closer to the desired output.

The backpropagation algorithm is based on the idea of gradient descent. The weights are adjusted in the direction that minimizes the error. The error is measured by the difference between the actual output of the network and the desired output.

The backpropagation algorithm is used in many different types of neural networks, including those used for pattern recognition and for predictions. It is a powerful algorithm that can learn complex relationships between the inputs and outputs.

Describe the difference between regression and classification problems in machine learning.

There are two main types of machine learning: regression and classification. Regression is used to predict continuous values, such as prices or weights. Classification is used to predict categorical values, such as labels or names.

Artificial intelligence is a branch of computer science that deals with creating intelligent machines. Machine learning is a subset of artificial intelligence that deals with creating algorithms that can learn from data and improve their performance over time.

What is the purpose of activation functions in neural networks?

Activation functions are used in neural networks in order to determine whether a neuron should be activated or not. This is done by mapping the input values to a range of 0 to 1. If the input value is greater than the threshold, then the neuron is activated and will fire. Otherwise, it will remain inactive.

The purpose of activation functions is to introduce non-linearity into the neural network. This is necessary in order to solve complex problems that cannot be solved by linear methods. Without activation functions, neural networks would only be able to learn linear relationships between input and output values.

The difference between artificial intelligence and machine learning is that artificial intelligence is a field of study that is concerned with creating intelligent agents. This involves creating algorithms that can learn and make decisions on their own. Machine learning, on the other hand, is a subset of artificial intelligence that is concerned with creating algorithms that can learn from data.

Explain the concept of a confusion matrix in classification models.

A confusion matrix is a table that is used to evaluate the performance of a classification model. The table is made up of four quadrants that represent the predicted and actual values for each class. The first quadrant represents the true positives, which are the cases where the model correctly predicted the positive class. The second quadrant represents the false positives, which are the cases where the model incorrectly predicted the positive class. The third quadrant represents the true negatives, which are the cases where the model correctly predicted the negative class. The fourth quadrant represents the false negatives, which are the cases where the model incorrectly predicted the negative class.

The accuracy of a classification model is the number of correct predictions divided by the total number of predictions. The accuracy can be calculated from the confusion matrix using the following formula:

Accuracy = (True Positives + True Negatives) / (True Positives + True Negatives + False Positives + False Negatives)

The precision of a classification model is the number of correct predictions divided by the total number of predictions made. The precision can be calculated from the confusion matrix using the following formula:

Precision = True Positives / (True Positives + False Positives)

The recall of a classification model is the number of correct predictions divided by the total number of cases in the data set. The recall can be calculated from the confusion matrix using the following formula:

Recall = True Positives / (True Positives + False Negatives)

The F1 score is a measure of a classification model's accuracy and precision. The F1 score can be calculated from the confusion matrix using the following formula:

F1 score = 2 * (Precision * Recall) / (Precision + Recall)

The concept of a confusion matrix is important in understanding the performance of classification models. The accuracy, precision, and recall measures can be used to compare different models and to choose the best model for a given data set.

How do you handle categorical variables in a machine learning model?

Artificial intelligence (AI) and machine learning (ML) are two very closely related fields of study. Both involve using computers to learn from data and make predictions or decisions.

However, there is a key difference between AI and ML. AI is focused on creating systems that can perform tasks that ordinarily require human intelligence, such as reasoning and natural language understanding. ML, on the other hand, is a subfield of AI that deals with creating algorithms that can learn from data and improve their performance over time.

One of the key challenges in ML is dealing with categorical variables. These are variables that can take on a limited number of values, such as "male" or "female". One way to deal with categorical variables is to use one-hot encoding. This is a process of converting the categorical variable into a vector of zeros and ones, where each value corresponds to a different category.

For example, if we have a categorical variable with three values (A, B, and C), we can one-hot encode it as follows:

A: [1, 0, 0]

B: [0, 1, 0]

C: [0, 0, 1]

One-hot encoding is a simple and effective way to deal with categorical variables in ML models. It can help the model to better learn from the data and make more accurate predictions.

What is the difference between bag-of-words and word embeddings in natural language processing (NLP)?

There are a few key differences between bag-of-words and word embeddings in natural language processing. Bag-of-words is a simpler approach that just looks at the frequency of words in a document, without taking into account any grammar or context. Word embeddings, on the other hand, try to represent words in a way that captures some of their meaning and context. This can be helpful for tasks like sentiment analysis, where the context of a word can be important.

When it comes to artificial intelligence and machine learning, there is a bit more overlap between the two fields. Both involve using computers to learn from data and make predictions. However, artificial intelligence generally refers to methods that are more complex and try to mimic human intelligence, while machine learning is a more general term that covers a range of methods, including some that are less complex.

Describe the concept of reinforcement learning and provide an example scenario.

The concept of reinforcement learning is based on the idea of providing positive reinforcement to encourage a desired behavior. For example, if a child is behaving well in school, they may be rewarded with a toy or a trip to the park. This type of reinforcement learning is often used in behavioral therapy to help people learn new, desired behaviors.

Machine learning is a type of artificial intelligence that allows computers to learn from data, without being explicitly programmed. For example, a machine learning algorithm might be used to automatically identify patterns in data.

How would you handle outliers in a dataset?

There are a few ways to handle outliers in a dataset. One way is to simply remove the outliers from the dataset. This is usually done if the outliers are not representative of the population that you are trying to model. Another way to handle outliers is to transform the data so that the outliers are not as extreme. This can be done by using a log transformation or by Winsorizing the data.

Explain the concept of k-fold cross-validation and its advantages.

When it comes to k-fold cross-validation, the data is first divided into k subsets. Then, the model is trained on k-1 subsets while the remaining subset is used for testing. This process is repeated until each subset has been used for testing. The advantages of k-fold cross-validation include that it is more reliable than using a single train/test split and that it reduces the chances of overfitting.

When it comes to artificial intelligence and machine learning, there is often a lot of confusion between the two terms. Artificial intelligence is a broader term that includes machine learning. Machine learning is a subset of artificial intelligence that deals with the ability of machines to learn from data.

What are the challenges of deploying machine learning models in production?

One of the key challenges of deploying machine learning models in production is the difference between artificial intelligence and machine learning. Artificial intelligence is a field of computer science and engineering focused on the creation of intelligent agents, which are systems that can reason, learn, and act autonomously. Machine learning, on the other hand, is a subset of artificial intelligence that deals with the creation of algorithms that can learn from and make predictions on data.

The challenge lies in the fact that artificial intelligence is often seen as a black box, while machine learning is more transparent. This can make it difficult to deploy machine learning models in production, as there is often a lack of understanding of how the models work and what they are trying to achieve. Additionally, machine learning models can be very complex, making them difficult to deploy and manage in production environments.

How would you deal with the curse of dimensionality in machine learning?

The curse of dimensionality is a well-known problem in machine learning. It occurs when the number of features in a data set is too high, and the data set becomes too sparse to be useful. This can happen when the data set is too large, or when the features are not well-chosen.

There are a few ways to deal with the curse of dimensionality. One is to choose a smaller data set, which will have fewer features and be less sparse. Another is to choose a different machine learning algorithm that is less susceptible to the curse of dimensionality. Finally, you can try to reduce the dimensionality of the data set by using feature selection or feature extraction techniques.

Describe the difference between batch gradient descent and stochastic gradient descent.

Batch gradient descent is an optimization algorithm that updates the weights of the model after each iteration by calculating the gradient of the error with respect to the weights. The weights are updated in the direction that minimizes the error.

Stochastic gradient descent is an optimization algorithm that updates the weights of the model after each iteration by calculating the gradient of the error with respect to the weights. The weights are updated in the direction that minimizes the error. However, in stochastic gradient descent, the gradient is calculated for each training example, rather than for the entire training set. This makes stochastic gradient descent much faster than batch gradient descent.

What is the purpose of a validation set in machine learning?

A validation set is used in machine learning to assess the performance of a model on unseen data. It is important to have a validation set because it allows you to tune your model and avoid overfitting on the training data.

The purpose of a validation set is to provide a unbiased assessment of the model's performance. The difference between artificial intelligence and machine learning is that artificial intelligence is a broader field that includes machine learning. Machine learning is a subset of artificial intelligence that focuses on the development of algorithms that can learn from data.

Explain the concept of hyperparameter tuning and methods used for it.

Hyperparameter tuning is the process of optimizing a model by fine-tuning its hyperparameters. Hyperparameters are the parameters that govern the training process of a machine learning model, such as the learning rate, the number of hidden layers, or the regularization parameter.

There are a few different methods that can be used for hyperparameter tuning, such as grid search, random search, or Bayesian optimization. Grid search is the process of exhaustively searching over a given grid of hyperparameter values, while random search randomly samples values from a given distribution of hyperparameter values. Bayesian optimization is a more sophisticated approach that uses a Bayesian model to predict the optimal hyperparameter values.

Hyperparameter tuning is important because it can help a machine learning model to generalize better to new data. If a model is overfit to the training data, it will perform poorly on unseen data. By tuning the hyperparameters, we can help the model to find a better balance between fitting the training data and generalizing to new data.

How would you handle a situation where your machine learning model is overfitting the training data?

If your machine learning model is overfitting the training data, you can try to increase the size of the training data set, or use a different model.

Describe the purpose and functioning of a support vector machine (SVM).

A support vector machine is a supervised machine learning algorithm that can be used for both classification and regression tasks. The algorithm is trained on a dataset of labeled examples, where each example is a vector of features (attributes) and a label. The labels can be either categorical (e.g. class A or class B) or real-valued (e.g. 1.0 or 2.0). The goal of the SVM algorithm is to find the best decision boundary (or hyperplane) that separates the examples with different labels.

The decision boundary is defined by a set of support vectors, which are the examples that are closest to the boundary. The position and orientation of the decision boundary is determined by the support vectors. The SVM algorithm tries to maximize the margin, which is the distance between the decision boundary and the closest support vectors.

The SVM algorithm can be used for both linear and non-linear classification. For linear classification, the decision boundary is a hyperplane. For non-linear classification, the decision boundary is a non-linear curve. The SVM algorithm can also be used for regression tasks, where the goal is to predict a real-valued output.

The difference between artificial intelligence and machine learning is that artificial intelligence is a broader field that includes machine learning. Artificial intelligence also includes other subfields such as natural language processing and computer vision. Machine learning is a subset of artificial intelligence that focuses on the development of algorithms that can learn from data.

What are the steps involved in data preprocessing for a machine learning model?

Artificial intelligence (AI) and machine learning (ML) are often used interchangeably, but there is a big difference between the two. AI is a broad field that includes many different subfields, such as natural language processing (NLP), computer vision, and robotics. ML is a subset of AI that focuses on the development of algorithms that can learn from and make predictions on data.

Data preprocessing is a critical step in the development of any machine learning model. The goal of data preprocessing is to clean and transform the data so that it can be used by the ML algorithm. This step is often referred to as data wrangling.

There are four main steps in data preprocessing:

1. Data cleaning: This step involves identifying and removing any invalid or missing data. This is important because invalid data can skew the results of the ML algorithm.

2. Data transformation: This step involves transforming the data into a format that can be used by the ML algorithm. This may involve scaling

the data, converting categorical data to numerical data, or creating new features from existing data.

3. Data split: This step involves splitting the data into two sets: a training set and a test set. The training set is used to train the ML algorithm, while the test set is used to evaluate the performance of the algorithm.

4. Data normalization: This step involves normalizing the data so that it is within a specific range. This is important because some ML algorithms require data to be within a certain range in order to function properly.

Explain the concept of collaborative filtering in recommendation systems.

Collaborative filtering is a method of making recommendations that is based on the collective wisdom of a group of people. This approach relies on the fact that people are more likely to trust the recommendations of others who share their tastes and preferences.

Machine learning is a subset of artificial intelligence that focuses on the ability of computers to learn from data. This approach to AI is based on the idea that computers can be trained to recognize patterns and make predictions.

How do you handle time series data in machine learning?

There are a few key ways to handle time series data in machine learning. One is to simply treat the data as though it were a regular dataset - this can work well for some models, but may not be ideal for others. Another way is to use a sliding window, which allows you to take into account previous data points when making predictions. This can be especially useful for time series data that may have trends or patterns. Finally, you can also use a recurrent neural network (RNN), which is designed specifically for handling time series data.

When it comes to the difference between artificial intelligence and machine learning, it is important to note that artificial intelligence is a broader field that includes machine learning. Machine learning is a subset of artificial intelligence that focuses on the ability of machines to learn from data. Artificial intelligence can also include things like natural language processing and computer vision, which are not necessarily related to learning.

Describe the concept of decision trees and how they are used in machine learning.

Decision trees are a type of machine learning algorithm that are used to create a model that can predict an outcome based on a set of input data. Decision trees are used in a variety of applications, such as predicting the price of a stock or the probability of a person defaulting on a loan.

The main difference between artificial intelligence and machine learning is that artificial intelligence is a broader field that includes machine learning. Artificial intelligence is concerned with creating intelligent systems that can perform tasks that would normally require human intelligence, such as understanding natural language and recognizing objects. Machine learning, on the other hand, is a subfield of artificial intelligence that focuses on creating algorithms that can learn from data and improve their performance over time.

What is the purpose of dropout in neural networks?

The purpose of dropout in neural networks is to prevent overfitting. Overfitting occurs when a model is too closely fit to the training data, and does not generalize well to new data. Dropout randomly "drops out" (removes) a number of nodes from the network during training, which forces the network to learn to function without those nodes. This prevents the network from overfitting, and allows it to generalize better to new data.

The difference between artificial intelligence and machine learning is that artificial intelligence is a broader field that includes machine learning. Machine learning is a subset of artificial intelligence that focuses on the development of algorithms that can learn from data.

Explain the concept of clustering and different clustering algorithms.

Clustering is a technique for grouping data points so that points within a group are more similar to each other than points in other groups. Clustering is often used for exploratory data analysis to find hidden patterns in data. There are a variety of clustering algorithms, each with its own strengths and weaknesses.

Artificial intelligence (AI) is a branch of computer science that deals with creating intelligent machines that can reason, learn, and act autonomously. AI research deals with the question of how to create computers that are capable of intelligent behaviour.

Machine learning is a subset of AI that deals with the question of how to create computer systems that can learn from data. Machine learning algorithms are used to automatically improve the performance of a system on a given task by increasing its ability to learn from data.

How would you handle a situation where your machine learning model is underfitting the training data?

If you find that your machine learning model is underfitting the training data, there are a few possible ways to address the issue. One option is to try a different model altogether. This could mean using a different algorithm or changing the model's parameters. If you think the issue might be with the data itself, you could try pre-processing the data in a different way or increasing the amount of data. Finally, it could be that the problem is with the way the features are defined. In this case, you would need to go back and review the feature engineering process.

What is the role of activation functions in neural networks?

Activation functions are important in neural networks because they help to determine how a neuron will fire in response to input. There are a variety of activation functions, and which one is used can make a big difference in the performance of a neural network.

The role of activation functions is to introduce non-linearity into the network. This is important because linear models are often too simplistic to model real-world data. By using activation functions, we can make neural networks that are better able to learn complex patterns.

There are a number of different activation functions, and each has its own strengths and weaknesses. The most popular activation function is the sigmoid function, which is good at modeling binary data. However, sigmoids can cause problems when training neural networks because of the way they squash input values.

Other activation functions include the tanh function, which is similar to the sigmoid function but avoids some of the problems associated with sigmoids. The ReLU function is another popular choice, which is fast to compute and often works well in practice.

The choice of activation function can have a big impact on the performance of a neural network. It is important to experiment with different activation functions to find the one that works best for your data and your task.

Describe the difference between online
learning and batch learning.

There is a big difference between online learning
and batch learning. With online learning, the
model is trained on individual data points one at a
time. This is different from batch learning, where
the model is trained using a batch of data points all
at once.

Artificial intelligence is a branch of computer
science that deals with creating intelligent
machines that can think and work like humans. On
the other hand, machine learning is a subset of
artificial intelligence that deals with the creation of
algorithms that can learn from data and improve
their performance over time.

How would you handle a situation where your machine learning model suffers from high bias?

If your machine learning model suffers from high bias, there are a few things you can do to try and improve it. First, you can try to increase the amount of data that you're training the model on. More data can help the model learn the underlying patterns better and reduce bias. Second, you can try different model architectures or hyperparameter values to see if that makes a difference. Sometimes a small change can make a big difference in reducing bias. Finally, you can try to pre-process the data in a way that reduces bias. This might involve removing outliers or transforming the data in some way.

Explain the concept of transfer learning and when it is beneficial.

Transfer learning is a machine learning technique where knowledge learned in one domain can be applied to another domain. This is beneficial when there is a shortage of data in the target domain, or when the target domain is different from the source domain but there is some similarity between them. For example, if we want to build a machine learning model to recognize faces, we can use a model that has already been trained on a large dataset of faces. This model can then be fine-tuned on a smaller dataset of faces from the target domain.

Artificial intelligence is a field of computer science that deals with creating intelligent agents, which are systems that can reason, learn, and act autonomously. Machine learning is a subfield of artificial intelligence that deals with creating algorithms that can learn from data and improve their performance over time.

What is the difference between a generative model and a discriminative model?

There are two main types of models for machine learning: generative and discriminative. Generative models learn the joint probability distribution of the input and output variables, while discriminative models learn the conditional probability distribution of the output given the input.

The main difference between artificial intelligence and machine learning is that artificial intelligence can be used to create programs that can make decisions on their own, while machine learning is a subset of artificial intelligence that focuses on creating programs that can learn from data.

Describe the concept of LSTMs (Long Short-Term Memory) in recurrent neural networks.

LSTMs are a type of recurrent neural network that are designed to capture long-term dependencies in data. This is done by using a memory cell that can remember information for long periods of time, and by using gates that control the flow of information into and out of the cell.

LSTMs are often used for tasks such as machine translation, where the meaning of a sentence can depend on the context of the entire document. They are also used for time series prediction, where past data can be used to predict future trends.

Artificial intelligence is a field of computer science that deals with creating intelligent agents, which are systems that can reason and make decisions on their own. Machine learning is a subfield of AI that deals with creating algorithms that can learn from data and improve their performance over time.

How would you evaluate the performance of a regression model?

There are many ways to evaluate the performance of a regression model. One way is to look at the coefficient of determination, which tells us how much of the variation in the dependent variable is explained by the independent variable. Another way to evaluate the performance of a regression model is to look at the root mean squared error, which tells us how close the predicted values are to the actual values.

Made in the USA
Middletown, DE
16 October 2023

40936142R00035